Timeless Quotes
Quips
and
Wise Sayings

Timeless Quotes
Quotes
Quips
and
Wise Sayings

Jim Redman

Copyright © 2017, 2018 by Jim Redman.

All rights reserved. Except as provided by U.S. and international copyright laws, no part of this publication may be reproduced, stored in a retrieval system or transmitted in any form or by any means without the prior written permission of the author, except for use of brief quotations in a review or journal.

ISBN: 978-1543275544

Fourth Edition, Rev. April 2018

INTRODUCTION

Most people have a real fondness for quotes; that is ones that are moving, or funny or seem to accurately express in a neat phrase some universal truth about the human condition.

The following collection is an eclectic assortment that represents commentary, wisdom and opinion expressed by personalities down the ages. The authors include notables as well as ordinary people. Also represented are pronouncements by some of history's most controversial figures. The entries may be viewed by individual readers as sometimes touching, perhaps amusing, often provocative. They are loosely arranged in the broad categories of *Everyday Life, Philosophy and Religion, Politics and Government, War and Conflict, History and Science, Business and Commerce*; although many if not most of the entries could properly be placed in more than one category.

A word about sources. Where possible the actual source work of the quote is given; in other cases only the author is shown; finally many anonymous quotes have simply long been part of public folklore. Apologies are given for any oversight or omissions in this regard.

Special credit to Jim Fisk and Robert Barron, authors of *The Official MBA Handbook* and *Great Business Quotations* whose selection of quotations is always right on target.

Jim Redman
email: jim@corpplan.com

Fourth Edition, Rev. April 2018

CONTENTS

1	Everyday Life	1
2	Philosophy and Religion	27
3	Politics and Government	51
4	War and Conflict	75
5	History and Science	91
6	Business and Commerce	101
	The Author	115

1

Everyday Life

"Life is tough, but made tougher by stupidity."
-- John Wayne

"Not everything that is faced can be changed, but nothing can be changed until it is faced."
-- Brandi Harless

"It's hard to make a comeback when you haven't been anywhere."
-- Bob Sendall

"Her nagging is a sign that she cares. Silence means she's plotting your death."
-- Anon

"There are only three days that really matter – yesterday, today and tomorrow."
-- Anon

"The trouble with giving advice is that the wise don't need it and the foolish won't heed it."
-- Anon

"There is nothing more fatiguing than the eternal facing of an uncompleted task."
-- William James

"I'm done with doctors! I note that everyone who died in this town last year had medical attention."
-- Heinrich Heine

"Keep your words sweet - you never know when you might have to eat them."
-- Anon

"You can burn a candle at both ends if it is long enough."
-- Albert Schweitzer

"Do I contradict myself?
Very well then I contradict myself;
I am large. I contain multitudes."
-- Walt Whitman, *Song of Myself*

"Go little where wanted; go not at all where little wanted."
-- Georgia Frontiere

Timeless Quotes

"If all you ever do is all you've ever done, then all you'll ever get is all you ever got."
-- Georgia Frontiere

"Don't waste time learning the 'tricks of the trade.' Instead, learn the trade."
-- H. Jackson Brown

"Beware of the person who has nothing to lose."
-- H. Jackson Brown

"It takes twenty years to make an overnight success."
-- Eddie Cantor

"Be brave. Even if you're not, pretend to be. No one can tell the difference."
-- H. Jackson Brown

"Success is simply a matter of luck. Ask any failure."
-- Earl Wilson

"The worst part of having success is finding someone who is happy for you."
-- Bette Midler

"Never deprive someone of hope; it might be all he or she has."
-- H. Jackson Brown

"Never pay for work before it's completed."
 -- H. Jackson Brown

"Good judgment comes from experience; experience comes from bad judgment."
-- Mulla Nasrudin

"Learn to say no politely, firmly and quickly."
-- H. Jackson Brown

"When you look back on life, you'll regret the things you didn't do more than the ones you did."
 -- H. Jackson Brown

"Even lack of baggage is baggage."
-- Anon

"If someone criticizes you, see if there is any truth to what he is saying; if so, make changes. If there is no truth to the criticism, ignore it and live so that no one will believe the negative remark."
-- Anon

"It isn't what you know that counts, it's what you can think of in time."
-- Anon

"Never tell a lie...unless lying is one of your strong points."
-- George Plunkitt

"If you don't agree with me, it means you haven't been listening."
-- Sam Markewich

"Money does make all the difference. If you're rich and have two jobs, you have diversified interests. If you're poor and have two jobs, you're moonlighting."
-- Anon

"The rich may not live longer, but it certainly seems so to their poor relatives."
-- Anon

"Gentility is what is left over from rich ancestors after the money is gone."
-- John Ciardi

"Wealth: any income that is at least 10% more a year than the income of one's wife's sister's husband."
-- H.L. Mencken

"There is nothing more demoralizing than a small but adequate income."
-- Edmund Wilson

"A poor person who is unhappy is in a better position than a rich person who is unhappy. Because the poor person has hope. He thinks money would help."
-- Jean Kerr

"Money sometimes makes fools of important persons, but it may also make important persons of fools."
-- Walter Winchell

"Money can't buy friends but it can get you a better class of enemies."
-- Spike Milligan

"Money is exactly like sex: you think of nothing else if you don't have it, and other things if you do."
-- James Baldwin

"I've got all the money I'll ever need if I die by four o'clock."
-- Henny Youngman

"From birth to age eighteen, a girl needs good parents. From eighteen to thirty-five she needs good looks. From thirty-five to fifty-five, she needs a good personality. From fifty-five on she needs good cash."
-- Sophie Tucker

"I should like to live like a poor man, with a great deal of money."
-- Pablo Picasso

"Buy old masters. They fetch a much better price than old mistresses."
-- Lord Beaverbrook

"If you pick up a starving dog and make him thrive, he will not bite you. This is the principal difference between a dog and a man."
-- Mark Twain

"Always trust your gut. It knows what your head hasn't figured out yet."
-- Anon

"Don't try to memorize anything that you can look up."
-- Albert Einstein

"Even if you're on the right track, you'll get run over if you just sit there."
-- Will Rogers

"Behind of every achievement is a proud wife and a surprised mother-in-law."
-- Brooks Hays

"When you win, nothing hurts."
-- Joe Namath

"Show me a good loser and I'll show you a loser."
-- Jimmy Carter

"She's the kind of girl who climbed the ladder of success, wrong by wrong."
-- Mae West

"What really flatters a man is that you think him worth flattering."
-- George Bernard Shaw

"Pay attention to your enemies, for they are the first to discover your mistakes."
-- Antisthenes

"Make promises sparingly and keep them faithfully."
-- Anon

"Act quickly, think slowly."
-- Greek proverb

"We judge ourselves by what we feel capable of doing, while others judge us by what we have already done."
-- Henry Wadsworth Longfellow

"The people who get on in this world are the people who get up and look for the circumstances they want, and, if they can't find them, make them."
-- George Bernard Shaw

"Character is what you are in the dark."
-- Dwight L. Moody

"The first sign of intelligence is silence."
-- Anon

"Tact is the art of making a point without making an enemy."
-- Anon

"All work and no play makes Jack a dull boy."
-- Anon

"All play and no work makes jack."
-- Anon

"Correction does much, but encouragement does more. Encouragement after censure is as the sun after a shower."
-- Goethe

"Think like a man of action; act like a man of thought."
-- Henri Bergson

"The goal of criticism is to leave the person with the feeling that he or she has been helped."
-- Anon

"You must experience failure to appreciate success."
-- Chinese proverb

"Problems are the weeds of life – to be mowed down by some or to rise up and strangle others."
-- Anon

"Nothing is impossible for the person who doesn't have to do it."
-- Anon

"Tell me who's your friend, and I'll tell you who you are."
-- Russian proverb

"My tastes are aristocratic, my actions democratic."
-- Victor Hugo

"Be as a bird perched on a frail branch that she feels bending beneath her, still she sings away all the same, knowing she has wings."
-- Victor Hugo

"Common sense is misnamed – it is very uncommon."
-- Anon

"Initiative is doing the right thing without being told."
-- Victor Hugo

"Forty is the old age of youth; fifty the youth of old age."
-- Victor Hugo

"Adversity makes men, and prosperity makes monsters."
-- Victor Hugo

"When a man is out of sight, it is not too long before he is out of mind."
-- Victor Hugo

"Whenever a man's friends begin to complement him about looking young, he may be sure that they think he is growing old."
-- Victor Hugo

"The greatest happiness in life is the conviction that we are loved; loved for ourselves, or rather, loved in spite of ourselves."
-- Victor Hugo

"Strong and bitter words indicate a weak cause."
-- Victor Hugo

"Love all, trust a few. Do wrong to none."
-- William Shakespeare

"Love: A temporary insanity cured by marriage."
-- Ambrose Bierce

"Man will do many things to get himself loved, he will do all things to get himself envied."
-- Mark Twain

"He that falls in love with himself will have no rivals."
-- Benjamin Franklin

"People need loving most when they deserve it the least."
-- John Harrigan

"A woman begins by resisting a man's advances and ends by blocking his retreat."
-- Oscar Wilde

"Pain is temporary. Quitting lasts forever."
 -- Lance Armstrong

"Advice is what we ask for when we already know the answer but wish we didn't."
-- Erica Jong

"If it doesn't matter who wins or loses why do we keep score?"
-- Vince Lombardi

"Doubt can only be erased by action."
-- Goethe

"They may forget what you said, but they will never forget how you made them feel."
-- Carl W. Buechner

"My idea of an agreeable person is a person who agrees with me."
-- Benjamin Disraeli

"You always pass failure on the way to success."
-- Mickey Rooney

"Never worry about your heart until it stops beating."
-- Anon

"If things came easily in this life, we would never feel pride in our achievements."
-- Sara Paretsky

"Either you think you can or think you can't, either way you'll be right."
-- Henry Ford

"The measure of who we are is what we do with what we have."
-- Vince Lombardi

"The more chances you give someone the less respect they'll start to have for you. They'll begin to ignore the standards that you've set because they'll know another chance will always be given. They're not afraid to lose you

because they know no matter what you won't walk away. They get comfortable depending on your forgiveness. Never let a person get comfortable disrespecting you."
-- Chris Bridges

"Sometimes those who don't socialize much aren't actually anti-social, they just have no tolerance for drama and fake people."
-- Chris Bridges

"Give me six hours to chop down a tree and I will spend the first four sharpening the axe."
-- Abraham Lincoln

"There are no walls, no bolts, no locks that anyone can put on your mind."
-- Otto Frank

"To plant a garden is to believe in tomorrow."
-- Audrey Heyburn

"The doors of wisdom are never shut."
-- Benjamin Franklin

"You cannot push anyone up the ladder unless he is willing to climb."
-- Andrew Carnegie

"When you reach the end of your rope, tie a knot and hold on."
-- Franklin D. Roosevelt

"What gives you pleasure will also give you pain."
-- Mary Leonard

"Never trust a man who is a good dancer."
-- Mary Leonard

"There are four things necessary for a truly successful relationship:
1. Shared Values,
2. Shared Interests,
3. Shared Habits,
4. Physical Compatibility."
-- Ed Etess

"Even Buckingham Palace isn't big enough for two women."
-- Mary Leonard

"Never underestimate the seductive power of a good vocabulary."
-- Anon

"It is a good thing for an uneducated man to read books of quotations."
-- Winston Churchill

"It is not a lack of love, but a lack of friendship that makes unhappy marriages."
-- Freidrich Nietzsche

"When in doubt about continuing a relationship ask yourself, if the relationship ended tomorrow, would I be?
　1. Relieved
　2. Disappointed
　3. Not sure how I would feel
If the answer is relieved, get out now. If the answer is disappointed or not sure, take concrete steps to fix things before getting out."
-- Thomas Silver

"It's not that I'm afraid to die, I just don't want to be there when it happens."
-- Woody Allen

"The minute you start talking about what you are going to do if you lose, you have lost."
-- George Schultz

"A true friend is one who overlooks your failures and tolerates your successes."
-- Doug Larsen

"Try to learn something about everything and everything about something."
-- Thomas Henry Huxley

"Dream as if you'll live forever, live as if you'll die today."
-- James Dean

"Really great people make you feel that you, too, can become great."
-- Mark Twain

"Book love, my friends, is your pass to the greatest, the purest, and the most perfect pleasure that God has prepared for His creatures. It lasts when all other pleasures fade. It will support you when all other recreations are gone. It will last you until your death. It will make your hours pleasant as long as you live."
-- Anthony Trollope

"Here's to books, the cheapest vacation you can buy."
-- Charlaine Harris

"When I am reading a book, whether wise or silly, it seems to me to be alive and talking to me. Sometimes I read a book with pleasure, and detest the author. It is easy enough for a man to walk who has a horse at his command. The invalid is not to be pitied who has a cure up his sleeve. And such is the advantage I receive from books. They relieve me from idleness, rescue me from company I dislike, and blunt the edge of my grief, if it is not too extreme. They are the comfort and solitude of my old age. When I am attacked by gloomy thoughts, nothing

helps me so much as the running to my books. They quickly absorb me and banish the clouds from my mind. And they don't rebel because I use them only for lack of pastimes more natural and alive. They always receive me with welcome."
-- Montaigne

"Keep your fears to yourself; share your courage with others."
-- Robert Louis Stevenson

"It's better to deserve honors and not receive them, than to receive honors and not deserve them."
-- Anon

"It isn't enough to ask intelligent questions; you also have to listen intelligently to the answers."
-- Anon

"What can be done at any time will be done at no time."
-- Scottish proverb

"There are two things that are more difficult than making an after-dinner speech: climbing a wall which is leaning toward you and kissing a girl who is leaning away from you."
-- Winston Churchill

"She was already afraid she was over the hill and wasted a

good deal of energy fishing for compliments and then throwing them back because they were too small..."
-- Robert Littell *The Revolutionist*

"You must learn from the mistakes of others. You can't possibly live long enough to make all of them yourself."
-- Sam Levenson

"I started out with nothing and have most of it left."
-- Anon

"One gets one's heart's desire, but always a day too late and always a size too small..."
-- Kurt Tucholsky

"You can go a long way with a smile. You can go a lot farther with a smile and a gun."
-- Al Capone

"The Six Basic Human Emotions:
Happiness
Sadness
Anger
Fear
Surprise
Disgust"
-- Charles Darwin

"Success is getting what you want, happiness is wanting what you get."
-- W.P. Kinsella

"Whatever in life you know you should absolutely not do, don't ever do it the first time - because every time after that will be easier."
-- Anon

"When you see a couple having dinner together, and they are gazing into each other's eyes and enjoying animated conversation - what is the thing you know about them? - that they're not married."
-- Ed Etess

"A house without books is like a room without windows."
-- Horace Mann

"A friend is someone who knows all about you and still loves you."
-- Elbert Hubbard

"Always go to other people's funerals, otherwise they won't come to yours."
-- Yogi Berra

"I never learn anything talking. I only learn things when I ask questions."
 -- Lou Holtz

"Good friends are hard to find, harder to leave, and impossible to forget."
 -- Anon

"Nothing is impossible, the word itself says 'I'm possible'!"
-- Audrey Hepburn

"Choose a job you love, and you will never have to work a day in your life."
 -- Confucius

"Don't bother people for help without first trying to solve the problem yourself."
-- Colin Powell

"The trouble with being in the rat race is that even if you win, you're still a rat."
-- Lily Tomlin

"You only live once, but if you do it right, once is enough."
-- Mae West

"Speak when you are angry and you will make the best speech you'll ever regret."
-- Laurence J. Peter

"Keep your mind open and your mouth shut."
  -- Theodore Roosevelt

"Nobody who is really light-hearted behaves light-heartedly."
 -- Albert Speer

"Outside of a dog, a book is man's best friend. Inside of a dog, it's too dark to read."
-- Groucho Marx

"It's always darkest before things go black."
-- Mark Shields

"I can't change the direction of the wind, but I can adjust my sails to always reach my destination."
-- Jimmy Dean

"The minute you settle for less than you deserve, you get even less than you settled for."
-- Maureen Dowd

"You can do anything, but not everything."
-- David Allen

"No day is so bad it can't be fixed with a nap."
-- Carrie Snow

"Unacceptable minus consequences equals acceptable."
-- Anon

"Only weaklings suffer no criticism."
-- Edgar Jung

Timeless Quotes

"Vision without action is a daydream. Action without vision is a nightmare."
-- Japanese Proverb

"Feelings change - memories don't."
-- Joel Alexander

"In a dependent relationship the protégé can always control the protector by threatening to quit or leave."
-- Barbara Tuchman, *The March of Folly*

"No one is so sure of his premises as the man who knows too little."
-- Barbara Tuchman, *The March of Folly*

"Show the thing you contend for to be reason, show it to be common sense, show it to be the means of attaining some useful end, and then I am content to allow it what dignity you please."
-- Edmund Burke

"Manana does not mean tomorrow. It only means not today."
-- Anon

"... No matter how carefully a man may avoid women, they are apt to cause him trouble in the end ... "
-- John Gunther, describing Cecil Rhodes

"Never write it when you can say it, never say it when you can wink it, never wink it when you can nod it . . . "
-- Anon

"Your fences need to be horse-high, pig-tight and bull-strong.

Keep skunks and bankers at a distance.

Life is simpler when you plow around the stump.

A bumble bee is considerably faster than a John Deere tractor.

Words that soak into your ears are whispered...not yelled.

Forgive your enemies, it messes up their heads.

Meanness jes' don't happen overnight.

Do not corner something that you know is meaner than you.

It don't take a very big person to carry a grudge.

You cannot unsay a cruel word.

Every path has a few puddles.

When you wallow with pigs, expect to get dirty.

The best sermons are lived, not preached.

Most of the stuff people worry about ain't never gonna happen anyway.

Don't judge folks by their relatives.

Remember that silence is sometimes the best answer.

Live a good, honorable life...then when you get older and look back, you'll enjoy it a second time.

Don't interfere with something that ain't bothering you none.

Timing has a lot to do with the outcome of a rain dance.

If you find yourself in a hole, the first thing to do is stop diggin'.

Sometimes you get and sometimes get got.

The biggest troublemaker you'll probably ever have to deal with watches you from the mirror every mornin'.

Always drink upstream from the herd.

Lettin' the cat out of the bag is a whole lot easier than puttin' it back in.

If you get to thinkin' you're a person of some influence, try orderin' somebody else's dog around.

Don't pick a fight with an old man. If he is too old to fight, he'll just kill you.

Most times, it just gets down to common sense.

Live simply. Love generously. Care deeply. Speak kindly. Leave the rest to God.

-- Advice from an old farmer

2

Philosophy and Religion

"In a multiplicity of problems there is usually one master question, the settlement of which leads to solving the others."
-- Lord Cromer, quoted by John Buchan

"Human nature believes what it wants to believe . . . a gift which makes for happiness but not for truth."
-- John Buchan

"I believe in the courage of our soldiers and the skill and devotion of our leaders. I believe in the power of right, in the crusade of civilization, in our country, the eternal, the imperishable, the essential. I believe in confidence, in quiet thought, in the humble daily round, in discipline, in charity militant. I believe in the blood of wounds and the water of benediction; in the blaze of artillery and the flame of the votive candle; in the beads of the rosary. I believe in the hallowed vows of the old, and in the potent innocence

of children. I believe in women's prayers, in the sleepless heroism of the wife, in the calm piety of the mother, in the purity of our cause, in the stainless glory of our flag. I believe in our great past, in our great present, in our greater future. I believe in our countrymen, the living and the dead. I believe in the hands clenched for battle, and in the hands clasped for prayer. I believe in the reward of suffering, and the worth of hope. I believe in ourselves. I believe in God. I believe. I believe."
-- M. Henri Lavedan, *Le Credo Patriotique*, 1916

"Who looks outside, dreams, who looks inside, awakens."
-- Carl Jung

"Each morning sees some task begun,
    Each evening sees it close.
Something attempted, something done,
    Has earned a night's repose."
-- Henry Wadsworth Longfellow

"When a task has once begun,
    Never leave it 'till it's done.
Stand the labor big or small,
    Do it well or not at all."
-- Karen Burton-Hansen

"Those whom the gods wish to destroy they first call promising."
-- Cyril Connolly

"It is easier for a camel to get through the eye of a needle than for a rich man to enter the Kingdom of God."
-- Matthew, 19:24

"What surprises me most about humanity? Man, because he sacrifices his health to make money. Then he sacrifices money to recuperate his health. And then he is so anxious about the future that he does not enjoy the present; the result being that he does not live in the present or the future; he lives as if he is never going to die, and then dies having never really lived."
-- The Dalai Lama

"Idealism increases in direct proportion to one's distance from the problem."
-- John Galsworthy

"On the day a man is born his life is measured."
-- African proverb

"The roots of violence: Wealth without work; pleasure without conscience; knowledge without character; commerce without morality; science without humanity; worship without sacrifice; politics without principles."
-- Mahatma Gandhi

"We are all in the gutter, but some of us are looking at the stars."
-- Oscar Wilde

"Courage is resistance to fear, mastery of fear – not absence of fear."
-- Mark Twain

"A cat pent up becomes a lion."
 -- Italian proverb

"To know a man, observe how he wins his object, rather than how he loses it; for when we fail our pride supports us, when we succeed it betrays us."
 -- Charles Caleb Colton

"Do what thy manhood bids thee do
     from none but self expect applause,
He noblest lives and noblest dies
     who makes and keeps his self-made laws."
 -- Kasidah, Sir Richard Burton

"Man is the only animal that contemplates death, and also the only animal that shows any sign of doubt of its finality."
-- William Ernest Hocking

"Work spares us from three great evils: boredom, vice and want."
-- Voltaire

"If a man will not work, he shall not eat."
-- 2 Thessalonians 3:10

"Only those who dare to fail greatly can ever achieve greatly."
-- Robert F. Kennedy

"Change is the law of life. And those who look only to the past or present are certain to miss the future."
-- John F. Kennedy

"If all else fails, immortality can always be assured by spectacular failure."
-- John Kenneth Galbraith

"Don't be afraid to take a big step if one is indicated. You can't cross a chasm in two small jumps."
-- David Lloyd George

"They are poor discoverers who think there is no land when they can see nothing but sea."
-- Samuel Johnson

"A thought which does not result in an action is nothing much, and an action which does not proceed from a thought is nothing at all."
-- George Bernanos

"The feeble tremble before opinion, the foolish defy it, the wise judge it, the skillful direct it."
-- Mme. Jeanne Roland

"A life of action and danger moderates the dread of death. It not only gives us fortitude to bear pain, but teaches us at every step the precarious tenure on which we hold present being."
-- William Hazlett

"When water covers the head, a hundred fathoms are as one."
-- Persian proverb

"A timid person is frightened before a danger, a coward during the time, and a courageous person afterwards."
-- Jean Paul Richter

"Necessity makes even the timid brave."
-- Sallust

"Mystery magnifies danger as the fog the sun."
– Charles Caleb Colton

"The wise man in the storm prays to God not for safety from danger, but for deliverance from fear."
-- Ralph Waldo Emerson

"Death has but one terror, that it has no tomorrow."
-- Eric Hoffer

"To be alive at all involves some risk."
-- Harold Macmillan

"Do not seek death. Death will find you. But seek the road which makes death a fulfillment."
-- Dag Hammarskjold

"The last pleasure in life is the satisfaction of discharging our duty."
-- William Hazlett

"There is only one corner of the universe you can be certain of improving – and that's your own self."
-- Aldous Huxley

"A proud man counts his newspaper clippings; a humble man counts his blessings."
-- Fulton J. Sheen

"God loves the poor. That is why he made so many of them."
-- Anon

"A man who is not a liberal at sixteen has no heart. A man who is not a conservative at sixty has no head."
-- Benjamin Disraeli

"Chance is the pseudonym God uses when He'd rather not sign His own name"
-- Anatole France

"Ponder the life led by others long ago, the life that will be led after you, the life being led in uncivilized races; how many do not even know your name, how many will very soon forget it, and how many, who praise you perhaps now, will very soon blame you."
-- Marcus Aurelius

"Preserve the right of thy place and stir not questions of jurisdiction; rather assume thy right in silence and de facto than voice it with claims and challenges. Preserve likewise the rights of inferior places; and think it more honour to direct in chief than to be busy in all."
-- Francis Bacon

"Look to the Northward stranger,
    Just over the hillside there.
Have you ever in your travels seen,
    A land more passing fair?"
-- Epitaph of James Norman Hall

"If you planning for a year, sow rice. If you are planning for a decade, plant trees. If you are planning for a lifetime, educate people."
-- Chinese proverb

"When elephants fight, the grass always suffers."
-- Swahili saying

"When you were born, you cried and the world rejoiced. Live your life in such a way so that when you die, the world cries and you rejoice."
-- Indian proverb

"The death of an old person is like the loss of a library."
-- African proverb

"It is part of the cure to wish to be cured."
-- Latin proverb

"Everything being a constant carnival, there is no carnival left."
-- Victor Hugo

"An intelligent hell would be better than a stupid paradise."
-- Victor Hugo

"Courage is grace under pressure."
-- Ernest Hemingway

"Courage is the discovery that you may not win, and trying when you know you can lose."
-- Tom Krause

"We shall not cease from exploration
    And the end of all our exploring,
Will be to arrive where we started
    And know the place for the first time."
-- T.S. Eliot

"Ah, but a man's reach should exceed his grasp,
Or what's a Heaven for?"
-- Robert Browning

"Nothing is ever accomplished by a reasonable man."
-- Bucy's Law

"The optimist sees opportunity in every danger; the pessimist sees a danger in every opportunity."
-- Winston Churchill

"To laugh often and much;
  To win the respect of intelligent people and affection of children;
  To earn the appreciation of honest critics and endure the betrayal of false friends;
  To appreciate beauty, to find the best in others;
  To leave the world a bit better, whether by a healthy child, a garden patch, or a redeemed social condition;
  To know even one life has breathed easier because you have lived.
  This is to have succeeded."
-- Ralph Waldo Emerson

"Women are the guardians, keepers and protectors of the moral values of society. When they abdicate that responsibility, decay is the result."
-- Mary Leonard

"There have been things in my life that I admit I would do differently. Looking back on those 72 years I have lived, I can see all the mistakes I made and those I could have avoided. But I am deeply convinced that, in spite of all your mistakes and negligent behavior, if the line of your life still took you toward the goal you had set once and for all; if you were able to reach that goal, or at least get closer to it; if going in that direction you did not lose yourself, nor squander your strength, committed anything contemptible, humiliated yourself or climbed over dead bodies, nor harmed others to get there; if you were able to maintain the moral course within your soul which in every language is called conscience, you can consider your life a success..."
-- Klaus Fuchs

"The only Paradise is Paradise Lost."
-- Proust

"A moral policeman's lot is not a happy one, particularly when his own morality is in question."
-- John Toland

"In trouble to be troubled is to have your trouble doubled."
-- Daniel Defoe

"All progress depends on the unreasonable man."
-- George Bernard Shaw

"All generalizations are dangerous, even this one."
-- La Rochefoucauld

"Never risk the necessary in search of the superfluous."
-- Pushkin

"Even the educator must be educated."
 -- Karl Marx

"The evil that men do lives after them,
The good is oft interred with their bones."
-- William Shakespeare

"When you have eliminated the impossible, whatever remains, however improbable, must be the truth."
-- Sherlock Holmes

"The world respects the martinet but it reserves its affection for those who give it affection...It admits the need of efficiency, but it hates the efficient, for he is a constant rebuke to its own love of slack and slipshod ways, a constant menace to its comfortable rut of routine and custom."
-- A.G. Gardiner

"Courage is the first of the human qualities because it is the quality which guarantees all the others."
-- Winston Churchill

"A highly intelligent man should take a primitive and stupid woman."
-- Adolf Hitler

"Look down at me and you see a fool; look up at me and you see a god; look straight at me and you see yourself."
-- Charles Manson

"Everybody dies the death that corresponds to his character."
-- Benito Mussolini

"Great minds discuss ideas, average minds discuss events, small minds discuss people."
-- Eleanor Roosevelt

"Rules cannot take the place of character."
-- Alan Greenspan

"Education is the most powerful weapon which you can use to change the world."
-- Nelson Mandela

"Heroes may not be braver than anyone else. They're just braver five minutes longer."
-- Ronald Reagan

"Our intellect can function reliably only when it is removed from the influence of strong emotional impulses; otherwise it behaves merely as an instrument of the will and delivers the inference that the will requires . . . "
-- Sigmund Freud

"Narcissistic personalities are convinced of their special qualities and their superiority over others, and any threat to this self-image - such as being criticized, shown up or defeated - produces a violent reaction and often a desire for revenge . . . "
-- Sigmund Freud

"He who wants to live must fight, and he who does not want to fight in this world where eternal struggle is the law of life has no right to exist . . . "
-- Adolf Hitler

"A man who has been the undisputed favorite of his mother keeps for life the feeling of the conqueror, that confidence of success that often induces real success."
-- Sigmund Freud

"When you see something insurmountable ahead of you, say to yourself: 'All right! I am afraid. Now that I've been afraid, let's go forward!' "
-- Joan of Arc, quoted by Albert Speer

"All men are frightened. The more intelligent they are, the more they are frightened. The courageous man is the man who forces himself, in spite of his fears, to carry on."
-- George S. Patton Jr.

"Material is superior to the living, mortal human body, but it is not superior to the living and immortal human mind."
-- Hans von Seeckt

"His hatred of Christianity, however was directed toward the idea inherent in Christianity of an independent conscience answerable only to God; the command to obey God rather than man and to recognize a Kingdom that is not of this world . . . "
-- Friedrich Meinecke

"We ask but time to drift, to drift - and note the devious ways of man . . . "
-- George Pellew

"It is not the critic who counts, not the man who points out where the doer of deeds could have done them better. The credit belongs to the man in the arena, whose face is marred by dust and sweat and blood; who strives valiantly . . . who knows the great enthusiasms, the great devotions; who spends himself in a worthy cause; who at the best knows in the end the triumph of high achievement, and who at the worst, if he fails, at least fails while daring greatly, so that his place shall never be with those cold and timid souls who have known neither victory nor defeat."
-- Theodore Roosevelt

"Only those are fit to live who do not fear to die; and none are fit to die who have shrunk from the joy of life and the duty of life. Both life and death are part of the same Great Adventure . . . "
-- Theodore Roosevelt

"Narcissism, the term used to describe a psychological state in which the subject becomes so absorbed in himself that nobody and nothing else in the world is real by comparison. Narcissistic personalities are convinced of their special qualities and their superiority over others, and any threat to this self-image - such as being criticized, shown up, or defeated - produces a violent reaction and often a desire for revenge."
-- Alan Bullock

"Men believe in the truth of all that is seen to be strongly believed in."
-- Nietzsche

"What shall it profit a man, if he gains the whole world, and loses his soul?"
-- Jesus, Matthew 10:28

"Fate decides one half of our lives, the other half depends on ourselves."
  -- Machiavelli

"Poverty in time of trouble is something money can't buy."
-- Chinese proverb

"Man is a pliable animal who gets used to anything."
  -- Dostoevsky

"A discontented mind is like a serpent trying to swallow an elephant."
  -- Chinese proverb

"A clever man understands the meaning of a nod."
-- Chinese proverb

"Blessed are they who expect nothing, for they shall not be disappointed."
-- Eugene Debs

"My children, it is permitted you in time of grave danger to walk with the devil until you have crossed the bridge."
-- Orthodox Church proverb

"The inevitable course of fate overwhelms the wisest of human intentions."
-- Livy, *History of Rome*

"Grass grows over battlefields but never over gallows."
-- Anon

"Religious faith is like a tremendous mountain range. Tempting from a distance, but when you try to climb it you run into ravines, perpendicular walls, and stretches of treacherous glacier. Most climbers are forced to turn back; some plunge to destruction; but almost nobody reaches the peak. Yet the world from the top must offer a wonderfully novel and clean view."
-- Albert Speer, *The Spandau Diaries*

"The operation of a prison inevitably demoralizes the guards as well as the guarded."
-- Albert Speer

"One obtains power over a nightmare by calling it by its real name."
-- Albert Speer

"God? Religion? Terror is the best God. One sees that in the case of the Russians. Otherwise they wouldn't fight so."
-- Adolf Hitler

"For a man who has committed a wrong there is only one salvation: punishment. It is therefore better for him to suffer this punishment than to escape it; for to suffer it sustains his inner being."
-- Plato

"In general the dishonest more easily gain credit for being clever than the honest do for being good, men take pride in the one but are ashamed of the other . . . "
-- L. Sprague de Camp

"What is hell? It's 3 people locked forever in a small room - a lesbian, a gay, and a nymphomaniac . . . "
-- Sarte, Huis Clos

"A pious Indian was expected to go through four stages of life: first, a student, diligent and chaste; then a householder, begetting sons to carry on his line; then a holy hermit living in the forest; lastly, having broken all earthly ties, a homeless wanderer . . . "
-- L. Sprague de Camp, *Cities of the Ancient World*

"Mundus vult deipi."
-- Latin, the World wants to be deceived

"All religions differ within themselves according to the educational and economic levels of their practitioners. On the higher levels they tend to be monotheistic, intellectual and abstract, concerned with moral principles and shading off into philosophy. On the lower levels, they tend to be polytheistic, emotional, and concrete, concerned with the practical benefits to be had from rites and ceremonies and shading off into magic . . . "
-- L. Sprague de Camp, *Cities of the Ancient World*

"Existence is misery: Birth is pain, life is pain, and death is pain. Nor is death the end of misery, because one is reborn into another body, to begin anew the wretched round of existence. The cause of misery is desire, which in the nature of things always extends beyond what can be satisfied and is therefore thwarted. The main forms of desire are the cravings for sensuous pleasure, for wealth, and for personal immortality. To escape misery, one must extinguish desire. This is done by following the eightfold path: right views, right intention, right speech, right action, right occupation, right effort, right alertness, and right concentration. By practicing these virtues, one at last achieves Nirvana."
-- Buddhist creed, summarized by L. Sprague de Camp

"If you don't think the creator of this world is an incompetent bungler, just look around you . . . "
-- Gnostic saying

"Time in its irresistible and ceaseless flow carries along all created things, and drowns them in the depths of obscurity, no matter if they be quite unworthy of mention, or most noteworthy and important . . . "
-- Commena

"Tantum religio potuit sua dere malorum." Latin, such are the crimes to which religion leads.
-- Lucretius, commentary on book burning and evil of dogmatic theology

"Before we understand science, it is natural to believe that God created the universe. But now science offers a more convincing explanation . . . I believe the universe is governed by the laws of science; God does not intervene to break the laws. The laws of physics can explain the universe without the need for a creator; no one created the universe and no one decides our fate. There is probably no heaven and no afterlife . . . that is a fairy story for people who are afraid of the dark."
-- Stephen Hawking, 1942-2018, Director of Theoretical Cosmology Centre, University of Cambridge

"In the search for meaning we must not forget that the gods (or God, for that matter) are a concept of the human

mind; they are the creatures of man, not vice versa. They are needed and invented to give meaning and purpose to the puzzle that is life on earth, to explain strange and irregular phenomena of nature, haphazard events and, above all, irrational human conduct. They exist to bear the burden of all things that cannot be comprehended except by supernatural intervention or design."
-- Barbara Tuchman, *The March of Folly*

"To create solid and stable conviction there must be something that appeals to the eye. A faith sustained only by doctrine will never be anything but feeble and vacillating. If the authority of the Holy See were visibly displayed in majestic buildings, all the world would accept and revere it."
-- Pope Nicholas V, 1455, on the rebuilding of Rome

"Islam lacks spiritual originality and is not a religion with profound thoughts on God and the world . . . It has preserved all the instincts of the primitive religious mind and is thus able to offer itself to the uncivilized and half-civilized peoples of Asia and Africa as form of monotheism most easily accessible to them . . . Islam can be called a world religion only by virtue of its wide extension."
-- Albert Schweitzer

"Islam alone of the missionary faiths has not withered in the land of its birth, and once the religion of the Prophet has entirely conquered a country it has never yet been ejected therefrom."
-- Alan H. Broderick

"By my truth, I care not; a man can die but once; we owe God a death and let it go which way it will, he that dies this year is quit for the next."
-- William Shakespeare

"All thinking men must renounce the attempt to explain the universe."
-- Albert Schweitzer

"The great secret of success is to go through life as a man who never gets used up."
-- Albert Schweitzer

"Whosoever would save his life shall lose it, and whosoever shall lose his life for My sake shall save it."
-- Jesus

"Whatever is reasonable is good. To be truly rational is to become ethical."
-- Albert Schweitzer

"When we try to pick out anything by itself, we find it hitched to everything else in the universe."
-- John Muir

"It is not in the pursuit of happiness that we find fulfillment, it is in the happiness of pursuit."
-- Denis Waitley

3

Politics and Government

"A title won by the sword can only be held by the sword."
-- John Buchan

"It has long been a grave question whether any Government that is not too strong for the liberties of its people, can then be strong enough to maintain its existence in great emergencies."
-- Abraham Lincoln

"As to treaties, no people should sacrifice its existence on the altar of fidelity to treaty, but should only go so far as suits its own interests."
-- Bismarck

"All treaties are written with this clear understanding: so long as things remain as they are at present . . . "
-- Heinrich von Treitschke

"The law is mighty but necessity is mightier."
-- Goethe

"Strategy is a jealous mistress, who will not tolerate divided masters."
-- John Buchan

"No sane man wants to be without discipline and leaders."
-- John Buchan

"Being powerful is like being a lady. If you have to tell people you are, you aren't."
-- Margaret Thatcher

"The world will not rise to the occasion of solving the climate problem during this century because it is more expensive in the short run to solve the problem than it is to just keep acting as usual."
-- Jorgen Randers, *2052: A Global Forecast for the Next Forty Years*

"Forget committees. New, noble, world-changing ideas always come from one person working alone."
-- H. Jackson Brown

"I can make suggestions but I can decide nothing. I have plenty of influence but no power."
-- Sir John Dill, British liaison to U.S. Joint Chiefs WWII

"We Germans will never produce another Goethe, but we may produce another Caesar."
-- Oswald Spangler, 1925

"The art of leadership is saying no, not yes. It is very easy to say yes."
-- Tony Blair

"When dictatorship is a fact, revolution becomes a right."
-- Victor Hugo

"Liberation is not deliverance."
-- Victor Hugo

"The inherent vice of capitalism is the unequal sharing of blessings; the inherent vice of socialism is the unequal sharing of miseries."
-- Winston Churchill

"If a house be divided against itself, that house cannot stand."
-- Mark 3:25

"Truman's Law: If you can't convince them, confuse them."
-- Harry S. Truman

"The legitimate object of government is to do for the people what needs to be done, but which they can not, by individual effort, do at all, or do so well, for themselves."
-- Abraham Lincoln 1854

"Freedom is not worth having if it does not include the freedom to make mistakes."
-- Mahatma Gandhi

"Nearly all men can stand adversity, but if you want to test a man's character, give him power."
-- Abraham Lincoln

"Under the pretense of benefiting the people with the real object of securing the bondholders, our Government usurped the role over Egypt and suffered the consequences. Pity it is, our Government always goes against liberty of peoples, and favoring of autocrats. You may argue now, it is not a natural movement – that is said of all movements, even that made against Charles I, James II., etc., and it is the fashion to say it is only the agitators. Agitators are fruits of existing seeds. . ."
-- Charles Gordon, letter to Sir Samuel Baker, 1885

"In revolution, as in a novel, the most difficult part to invent is the end."
-- de Tocqueville

"Despotism tempered by assassination - that is our Magna Carta."
-- Russian saying

"A right delayed is a right denied."
-- Martin Luther King

"Dialogue, compromise, and negotiation are effective ways to solve problems and maintain national unity . . . "
-- Ronald Reagan, letter to Chun Doo Hwan, Korea President, 1989

"It is easier to run a revolution than a government."
-- Ferdinand Marcos

"Leadership in the Arab world is a role in search of an actor."
-- Nasser

"A ruling group is a ruling group so long as it can nominate its successors. The Party is [only] concerned with perpetuating itself . . ."
-- George Orwell

"To give the people a choice between candidates . . . designated by others is no democracy; especially when [in seeking] votes, these candidates try to outdo one another in promises that cannot be fulfilled."
-- Jerry Rawlings

"Naturally the common people don't want war...voice or no voice, the people can always be brought to the bidding of the leaders. That is easy. All you have to do is tell them they are being attacked, and denounce the peacemakers for lack of patriotism and exposing the country to danger. It works the same in every country."
-- Hermann Goring

"Iran can be governed like Switzerland only when Iranians behave like the Swiss."
-- Shan of Iran

"Paraguay will be torn by revolutions...that country will have to learn, like every other South American state, that a republic cannot succeed until it contains a certain body of men imbued with the principles of justice and honor."
-- Charles Darwin, 1839

"No one can achieve rapid development without concentrating wealth. You've got to make the cake bigger before you can start slicing it up."
-- Antonio Delfim Netto

"We are one family, one country with one nation, one government. And so we must have one party. It's that simple...we believe in the inexorable law of unity: you must be united or else you can be divided and perish."
-- Robert Mugabe

"There is nothing more difficult to carry out, nor more dangerous to handle, than to initiate a new order of things - for the reformer has enemies in all those who profit by the old order and only lukewarm defenders in all those who would profit by the new order . . . "
-- Niccolo Machiavelli

"The voluntary union of neighboring states by peaceful means is extremely rare. It is rare because, in such a union, the headman of one of the uniting states - normally the weaker of the two - stands to lose his job, and so do his supporters stand to lose theirs. They therefore resist the union, calling upon their subjects to preserve their 'liberty' and 'independence.' Contrariwise, a local leader in part of a larger nation, who feels that he is unlikely ever to attain supreme power in the nation, often starts a secessionist movement to form a new state with himself at the head. He exhorts his followers to strike for 'independence' and 'liberty' while the national leaders, who would lose power by secession, combat it by calling for 'loyalty' and 'unity'..."
-- L. Sprague de Camp

"Men must be caressed or annihilated; they will revenge themselves for small injuries, but cannot do so for great ones; the injury therefore that we do to a man must be such that we need not fear his vengeance."
-- Niccolo Machiavelli

"No matter what I say, people interpret it as it suits them."
-- Khomeni

"The seizure of power is only the beginning...the whole point is to retain power."
-- Stalin

"By means of shrewd lies, unremittingly repeated, it is possible to make people believe that heaven is hell - and hell heaven. The greater the lie, the more readily it will be believed."
-- Adolf Hitler

"If you build equality by increasing inequality, you'll be left with inequality; if you want to attain freedom by applying mass terror, the result will be mass terror; if you want to work for a just society through fear and repression, you will get fear and repression rather than universal fraternity . . . "
-- Leszek Kolakowski

"If you ask if I would prefer my people to be loyal out of fear or out of conviction - my answer is fear. Convictions can change but fear remains . . . "
-- Josef Stalin

Timeless Quotes

"One cannot keep by democratic institutions what one has acquired by force . . . "
-- Adolf Hitler

"Tyranny is a habit, it has a capacity for development, it develops finally into a disease. The human being and the citizen within the tyrant die forever; return to humanity, to repentance, to regeneration becomes almost impossible."
-- Dostoevsky, *The House of the Dead*

"Like a woman whose inner sensibilities are not so much subject to abstract reasoning but rather subject to a vague emotional longing for the strength that completes her being, and who would rather bow to a strong man than dominate a weakling - so the masses prefer a ruler to a suppliant . . . "
-- Adolf Hitler

"He who wills the end must also will the means . . . "
-- Lev Trotsky

"Aristotle long ago saw one of the ways tyranny is maintained - the creation of mistrust, for a tyrant is not overthrown until men begin to have confidence in one another . . . "
-- Alan Bullock

"The leader cannot be made, can in this sense also not be selected. The leader makes himself in that he comprehends the history (and destiny) of his people . . . "
-- Adolf Hitler

"Never tell people how to do things. Tell them what to do and they will surprise you with their ingenuity."
-- George S. Patton Jr.

"Nationalism, pushed to an extreme, just like sectarianism, destroys moral and even logical consciousness. Just and unjust, good and bad, true and false, lose their meaning - what men condemn as disgraceful and inhuman when done by others, they recommend in the same breath to their own people as something to be done to a foreign country."
-- Friedrich Paulsen

"'Our country, right or wrong!' This phrase, if given absolute acceptance is hideous and harmful in its consequences, because it pushes aside all moral limits in political transactions."
-- Friedrich Meinecke

"Democracy"
  -- from the Greek 'demos' (people) + 'kratein' (to rule)

"Because when you can make it evident that all men, big and small alike, have to obey the law, you are putting the safeguard of law around all men . . . "
-- Theodore Roosevelt

"Diplomacy is utterly useless where there is no force behind it; the diplomat is the servant, not the master, of the soldier . . . "
-- Theodore Roosevelt

"We have room for but one flag, the American flag - we have room for but one language here and that is the English language, for we intend to see that the crucible turns out people as Americans - and not as dwellers in a polyglot boarding house . . . "
-- Theodore Roosevelt

"Only say what must be said to him who must know it, and only when he must know it."
-- Adolf Hitler

"The Revolution, like Saturn, devours its children."
  -- Pierre Vergriand, Paris 1793

"They (some historic rulers) shared the same characteristic of turning aggression inwards and dividing the nation, instead of uniting it and directing aggression outwards."
  -- Alan Bullock

"There have been no cases in history where dying classes have departed from the scene voluntarily . . . "
  -- Josef Stalin

"A politician has his eye on the next election, and a statesman on the next generation."
  -- Field-Marshall Montgomery

"The function of a political leader in a democracy is not to impose his will, but to guide the people toward deciding wisely for themselves."
  -- Field-Marshall Montgomery

"Between two groups that want to make inconsistent kinds of worlds, I see no remedy except force."
  -- Oliver Wendell Holmes Jr.

"A leader cannot act to a degree beyond what the people will take; he must of course have courage, but if the people will not follow his decisions he will inevitably fail. He must therefore be a persuader . . . "
  -- Field-Marshall Montgomery

"Loyalty is a two-way street - you can't expect loyalty from those below you unless you yourself are loyal to your superiors."
  -- Field-Marshall Montgomery

"It is not the countries who lack the atom bomb or the big military who should be called 'second-rate powers', but the countries who lack the big ideals. Unlike the big military, big ideals have a way of surviving."
-- Field-Marshall Montgomery

"The three cardinal rules of covert operations: 1) Don't be found out, 2) If you are found out, don't admit it, 3) Always blame someone else."
-- Field-Marshall Montgomery

"There is no harm in saying the same thing over and over again, provided it is right."
-- Winston Churchill

"The hard fact is that all men are not created equal talent wise. Equality means equal access to the law and an equal right to justice under it."
-- Field-Marshall Montgomery

"Perfect equality of opportunity is impossible. However hard we may try, greater inequalities of capacity and therefore of opportunity will develop as children grow into men."
-- Field-Marshall Montgomery

"He had almost all the qualities needed for greatness in a democracy except the supreme one – character . . . "
-- Alkibiades of Athens, as described in *Cambridge Ancient History*

"Naked power - the form that government takes when people are not restrained by reverence, however irrational, for a royal dynasty, a religious doctrine, or a quasi-sacred constitution, then politics becomes an uninhibited, cutthroat scramble for unlimited power and privilege. Anything goes if it works . . . "
-- Bertrand Russell, *Power - A New Social Analysis*

"The trouble with being a king is that one has to kill so many people who have done nothing wrong, but whose mere existence is threatening to the state . . . "
-- Ptolemy II, paraphrased by L. Sprague de Camp

"While it may be true that people, en masse, always behave the same way other things being equal, the other things are never quite equal. . . "
-- L. Sprague de Camp

"Great minds have purposes, other minds have wishes."
-- Washington Irving

"The power which has always started the greatest religions and political advances in history rolling has from time immemorial been the magic power of the spoken word, and that alone. The broad masses of the people can be moved only by the power of speech. All great movements are popular movements, volcanic eruptions of human passions and emotional sentiments, stirred either by the cruel Goddess of Distress or by the firebrand of the word hurled among the masses; they are not the lemonade-like outpourings of the literary aesthetes and drawing-room heroes . . . "
-- Adolf Hitler

"Experts often possess more data than judgment."
-- Colin Powell

"Inept and corrupt regimes, like those of the terminal Romanovs or the Kuomintang, cannot generally be reformed short of total upheaval or dissolution."
-- Barbara Tuchman, *The March of Folly*

"Everything one has a right to do is not best to be done."
-- Benjamin Franklin

"The poorest man in his cottage may bid defiance to all the force of the Crown. It may be frail, its roof may shake; the wind may blow through it; the storms may enter - but the King of England cannot enter; all his forces dare not cross the threshold of the ruined tenement!"
-- William Pitt, 1763, speech in Parliament in protest of proposed search legislation

"Magnanimity in politics is often the truest wisdom, and a great empire and little minds go ill together."
-- Edmund Burke, 1775

"The price good men pay for indifference to public affairs is to be ruled by evil men."
-- Plato

"The attitude was a sense of superiority so dense as to be impenetrable. A feeling of this kind leads to ignorance of the world and of others because it suppresses curiosity."
-- Barbara Tuchman, *The March of Folly*, on British blunders in governing the American colonies.

"Confronted by menace, or what is perceived as menace, governments will usually attempt to smash it . . . but rarely to examine it, understand it, define it."
-- Barbara Tuchman, *The March of Folly*

"The symbol for those who manage the affairs of this country should be that of an overfed and overpetted dog, curled up cozily on a deep sofa, who lets out a sleepy growl whenever someone pulls its tail, but never troubles to open its eyes to see if the tail-puller is its master's son or a burglar."
-- Editorial by the *Malaya Tribune*, before Japanese invasion October 1941.

"You may exert power over them, but you can never govern an unwilling people."
-- Thomas Pownall, 1770

"Honor and dignity are not better served by persisting in a wrong measure once entered into, rather than rectifying an error as soon as it is discovered."
-- Benjamin Franklin

"Salvation is God's affair. Everything else belongs to me."
-- Friedrich Wilhelm I

"The highest form of religion is love the Fatherland more passionately than laws and princes, fathers and mothers, wives and children."
-- Ernst Moritz Arndt

"Not by speeches and majority votes are the great questions of the day decided, but by blood and iron."
-- Bismarck

"If you lie, lie big, for a little of even the most outrageous lie will stick if you press it hard enough. Never hesitate, never qualify, never concede a shred of validity or even decency to the other side. Attack, attack, attack!"
-- Adolf Hitler

"Whoever conquers the streets conquers the masses, and whoever conquers the masses conquers the state."
-- Adolf Hitler

"To establish control over such a vast nation must be vain, must be fatal. We shall be forced ultimately to retreat - let us retreat when we can, not when we must."
-- Lord Chatham, William Pitt, 1775

"The deterioration of every government begins with the decay of the principles on which it was founded."
-- Montesquieu, *Spirit of the Laws*

"Disgrace of a ruler is no great matter in world history, but disgrace of government is traumatic, for government cannot function without respect."
-- Barbara Tuchman, *The March of Folly*

"Problems and conflicts exist among other peoples that are not solvable by the application of American force or American techniques, or even American goodwill."
-- Barbara Tuchman, *The March of Folly*

"In the search for wiser government we should look for the test of character first. And the test should be moral courage."
-- Barbara Tuchman, *The March of Folly*

"There's no contradiction between a soft heart and a hard head."
-- Robert S. McNamara

"If you make nice with a tiger all it means is that you get eaten last."
-- Anthony Zucker

"When the British Commonwealth has to rule by force alone, it is finished."
-- British Kenyan official, quoted by John Gunther, *Inside Africa*

"It is dangerous to educate Africans. It will be more dangerous not to educate them."
-- Governor General of the Belgian Congo, quoted by John Gunther, *Inside Africa*

"South Africa is a country of black men – not white men. It has been so; it is so; and it will be so."
-- Anthony Trollope, 1877

"If you eat with them, you sleep with them."
-- John Gunther, on assimilation in Africa

"A proverb about Brazil in the slave trade days was that it was purgatory for a white man, hell for a Negro, and paradise for a mulatto."
-- John Gunther

"When a society values its philosophers more than its plumbers, it will find that neither its ideas nor its pipes hold any water."
-- Anon

"No Arab country will ever achieve true civilization until the women are emancipated."
-- John Gunther, *Inside Africa*

"People who live in deltas are apt to be soft...they are complacent by and large. These are the easiest people in the world to govern - if somebody *will* govern."
-- British official describing Egyptians, quoted by John Gunther, *Inside Africa*

"If it wasn't for myopia, we could see to Ethiopia."
-- Anon

"The police are the public, the public are the police. The police are only members of the public, who are paid to give full-time attention to duties which are incumbent on *every* citizen, in the interest of community welfare and existence."

-- Sir Robert Peel, Founder of the London Metropolitan Police

"All crime exists primarily in the mind. The law presumes the criminal intent for the wrongful act. The presumption of the law is that every person intends to do what he does, and intends the natural, necessary and probable consequences of his act. This presumption of law is open to be rebutted by evidence."
-- Chief Justice William F. Turner, Arizona Territory 1865

"Violators of law and good order are more deterred by the certainty than the severity of punishment."
-- Chief Justice Turner

"It is enough to say that the history of the world shows that material prosperity and happiness advance step by step with the advance of the people in virtue, intelligence and Christian civilization."
-- Chief Justice Turner

"A word about the relations between the whites and the blacks. What must be the general character of the intercourse between them? Am I to treat the black man as my equal or as my inferior? I must show him that I can respect the dignity of human personality in everyone, and ... the essential thing is that there shall be a real feeling of

brotherliness. How far this is to find complete expression in the sayings and doings of daily life must be settled by circumstances. The Negro is a child, and with children nothing can be done without the use of authority. We must, therefore, so arrange the circumstances of daily life that my natural authority can find expression. With regard to Negroes, then, I have coined the formula: 'I am your brother, it is true, but your elder brother . . . ' "
-- Albert Schweitzer

"The idea of the rights of man was formed and developed when society was an organized and stable thing. In a disorganized society the very well-being of man often demands that his fundamental rights be abridged."
-- Albert Schweitzer

"It is hard to keep oneself really humane."
-- Albert Schweitzer

"We prefer self-government with danger to servitude in tranquility."
-- Kwame Nkrumah

"Before we Christianize Africans, should we not Christianize ourselves?"
-- Denis Saurat

"Poor soil makes poor people, and poor people make poor soil worse."
-- R.L. Robb

"No government, no matter how infamous, can poison a whole people."
-- John Gunther

"My Motto is - Equal Rights for every civilised man south of the Zambesi. What is a civilised man? A man, whether white or black, who has sufficient education to write his name, has some property, or works. In fact, is not a loafer."
-- Cecil Rhodes

"Governments may think and act as .... force cannot be eliminated, and it is t......... nd unanswerable power. We are to........ e pen is mightier than the sword, but I know which o. these weapons I would choose."
-- Sir Adrian Carton de Wiart

"We in Poland do not recognize the concept of peace at any price. There is only one thing in the life of men, nations, and states that is without price, and this is honor."
-- Jozef Beck, 1938

"It is almost as difficult to get rid of an empire as to build one."
-- Anon

"Criteria for Sovereignty – a) a permanent population; b) a defined territory; c) an effective government; d) a capacity to enter into relations with other states."
-- National Lawyers Guild

"Civility and moderation are ultimately a matter of choice, not necessity. In the absence of a single source of coercion, all laws are simply codes of conduct rendered workable by mutual cooperation."
-- Robert O'Connell quoting Grotius, *Of Arms and Men*

4

War and Conflict

"We are now in a state of necessity, and necessity knows no law."
-- Theobald von Bethmann-Hollweg, German Chancellor on outbreak of World War I

"Most states have an army; the Prussian army is the only one that has a state."
-- Robert O'Connell, *Of Arms and Men*

"O God, assist our side; at least avoid assisting the enemy and leave the rest to me."
-- Prince Leopold of Anhalt-Dessau

"You are ordered abroad as a soldier of the King to help our French comrades against the invasion of a common enemy. You have to perform a task which will need your courage, your energy, your patience. Remember that the honour of the British Army depends upon your individual conduct. It will be your duty, not only to set an example of discipline and perfect steadiness under fire, but also to maintain the most friendly relations with those whom you are helping in this struggle. The operations in which you are engaged will, for the most part, take place in a friendly country, and you do your own country no better service than in showing yourself in France and Belgium in the true character of a British soldier. Be invariably courteous, considerate, and kind. Never do anything likely to injure or destroy property, and always look upon looting as a disgraceful act. You sure to be welcome and be trusted; your conduct must justify that welcome and that trust. Your duty cannot be done unless your health is sound. So keep constantly on guard against any excesses. In this new experience you may find temptations in wine and women. You must entirely resist both temptations, and while treating all women with perfect courtesy, you should avoid any intimacy.
Do your duty bravely.
Fear God.
Honour the King."
-- Lord Kitchener, address to soldiers of the BEF on the outbreak of war, 1914

"Heroes, you have taken two oaths – one to me, your king, and the other to your country. I am an old, broken man, on the edge of the grave, and I release you from your oath to me. From your other oath no one can release you. If you feel you cannot go on, go to your homes, and I pledge my word that after the war, if we come out of it, nothing shall happen to you.
But I and my sons stay here . . . "
-- Serbian King Peter I, address to troops on the eve of major battle, December 1914

"Under the orders of your devoted officers in the coming battle you will advance or fall where standing, facing the enemy. To those who fall I say:
You will not die, but will step into immortality. Your mothers will not lament your fate, but will be proud to have borne such sons. Your names will be revered forever and ever by your grateful country, and God will take you unto Himself."
-- Sir Arthur Currie, commander of Canadian Corps, address to the troops, battle of Lys, April 1918

"Never fight unless you have to –
Never fight alone –
Never fight for long . . . "
-- Brig. General Fox Connor

"War is the science of destruction."
-- John S.C. Abbott

"It is of no consequence if all the monuments ever created, all the pictures ever painted, and all the buildings ever erected by the great architects of the world were destroyed, if by their destruction we insure Germany's victory over her enemies."
-- Major General von Ditforth, Hamburg Nachrichten, November 1914

"Church Edict of 1139 outlawed the use of the crossbow against Christians - but not against Muslims."
-- Robert O'Connell, *Of Arms and Men*

"Hit your enemy in the belly, and kill him when he is down, and boil his prisoners in oil – if you take any – and torture his women and children. Then people will keep clear of you."
-- Admiral of the Fleet Lord Fischer, speaking at the Hague Peace Conference, 1898.

"If an injury has to be done to a man it should be so severe that his vengeance need not be feared."
-- Machiavelli

"Before war, military science seems a real science...like astronomy. After a war it seems like astrology."
-- Dame Rebecca West

"Men have been barbarians much longer than they have been civilized, and within us there is the propensity, persistent as the force of gravity, to revert under stress and strain, under neglect or temptation, to our first natures."
-- Walter Lippmann

"The first time is happenstance. The second time is coincidence. The third time is enemy action."
-- Anon

"Nothing is more difficult, and therefore more precious, than to be able to decide."
-- Napoleon

"Victory has a thousand fathers; defeat is an orphan."
-- Napoleon

"Victory is a mirage in the desert created by a long war."
-- B.H. Liddell Hart

"The impulse to mar and to destroy is as ancient and almost as nearly universal as the impulse to create. The one is an easier way than the other of demonstrating power."
-- Joseph Wood Krutch

"In preparing for battle I have always found that plans are

useless, but planning is indispensable."
-- Dwight D. Eisenhower

"My strategy is one against ten; my tactics, ten against one. "
-- Duke of Wellington at Waterloo

"An army is as brave as its privates and as good as its generals."
-- Anon

"The unforgivable crime in war is not making the wrong decision, but making no decision."
-- Frederick the Great

"The fewer men, the greater share of honor."
-- William Shakespeare, *Henry V*

"Peace is better than war, because in peace the sons bury their fathers, but in war the fathers bury their sons."
-- Croesus

"For every soldier war is the acid test, not only of his professional skill but of his character. The British Army traditionally placed the attributes of character above those of intellect. An officer could be a good soldier without being clever, but a clever officer was rarely a good soldier."
-- David Fraser

"If it will all be wonderful
    after the war,
Why didn't we have this old wo-er befo-er?"
-- A.P. Herbert, WWI soldier's ditty

"Sing me a song of a lad that is gone;
    Say, could that lad be I?"
-- R.L. Stevenson

"In the West the armies were too big for the country. In the East the country was too big for the armies."
-- Winston Churchill

"He who fights against the East fights against space."
-- Paul Herrmann

"Great Britain provided time; the United States provided money - and Soviet Russia provided blood."
-- Josef Stalin on Russian victory in World War II

"When you go home, tell them of us, and say,
For your tomorrow
We gave our today."
-- British War Memorial Inscription

"A single death is a tragedy, a million deaths are a statistic."
-- Josef Stalin

"War can only be abolished through war, and in order to get rid of the gun it is necessary to take up the gun."
-- Mao Tse-Tung

"Hurrah for revolution, and more cannon-shot!
A beggar upon horseback lashes a
    beggar on foot.
Hurrah for revolution and cannon
    come again!
The beggars have changed places,
    but the lash goes on."
-- W.B. Yeats, *The Great Day*

"Inter Arma Silent Leges."
-- Latin, "In time of war, the laws are silent."

"Exercitus facit imperatorum."
-- Latin, "The Army chooses the Ruler."

"Never in my life will I sign a declaration of war. I will always strike first . . . "
-- Adolf Hitler

"The victor will not be asked whether he told the truth. When starting and waging a war it is not right that matters, but victory."
-- Adolf Hitler

"War is for a man what childbirth is for a woman . . . "
-- Adolf Hitler

"One does not plan and then try to make circumstances fit the plan. One makes the plan fit the circumstances."
-- George S. Patton Jr.

"It may be that at some time in the dim future of the race the need for war will vanish; but that time is yet ages distant. As yet no nation can hold its place in the world, or can do any work really worth doing, unless it stands ready to guard its rights with an armed hand . . . "
-- Theodore Roosevelt

"If there is not the war, you don't get the great general; if there is not the great occasion, you don't get the great statesman; if Lincoln had lived in times of peace, no one would know his name now. . . "
-- Theodore Roosevelt

"A good commander is always careful to ensure that what is strategically desirable is also tactically possible with the forces at his disposal . . . "
-- Field-Marshall Montgomery

"War is the province of chance. In no sphere of human activity is such a margin to be left for this intruder."
-- von Clausewitz

"Battles are won primarily in the hearts of men - and when dealing with men justice is vital."
-- Field-Marshall Montgomery

"The infantrymen must be made to fear their officers more than the perils to which they are exposed."
-- Frederick the Great

"Simplicity, decision, and action - the hallmarks of military genius."
-- Field-Marshall Montgomery

"In war men are nothing. A man is everything."
-- Napoleon

"Superior force is a great persuader."
-- Winston Churchill

"If you're going to use military force, then you ought to use overwhelming military force . . . "
-- General Curtis Lemay

"Don't fight a battle if you don't gain anything by winning."
-- Erwin Rommel

"The enemy advances, we retreat. He camps we bother

him. He grows weary, we attack. He retreats, we pursue."
-- Mao Tse-Tung

"In war morale is worth three times as much as material."
-- Napoleon

"The British only win one battle - the last. They start with disasters but end with victory."
-- B.H. Liddell Hart

"Only the dead have seen the end of war."
-- Plato, 4th century BC

"He who seizes the initiative in war has won more than a battle."
-- von Ribbentrop

"There's always a war on. The difference is only whether the guns are firing or not. There's war in peacetime too."
-- von Ribbentrop

"Take calculated risks. That's different from being rash."
-- George H. Patton

"The time will come when the tension between the allies will become so great that a break will occur. All the coalitions in history have disintegrated sooner or later. The only thing is to wait for the right moment, no matter how hard it is. It is essential to deprive the enemy of his

belief that victory is certain - wars are finally decided by one side or the other recognizing that they cannot be won. We must allow no moment to pass without showing the enemy that, whatever he does, he can never count on our surrender. Never!"
-- Adolf Hitler

"American training and weapons could never supply the will to fight."
-- Barbara Tuchman, *The March of Folly*, describing ARVN setbacks

"In the final analysis it is their war. They are the ones who have to win it or lose it."
-- John F. Kennedy, 1963

"War is a procedure from which there can be no turning back without victory or acknowledging defeat."
-- Barbara Tuchman, *The March of Folly*

"The greatest contribution Vietnam is making . . . is developing an ability in the United States to fight a limited war without arousing public ire. . . . almost a necessity in our history, because this is the kind of war we'll likely be facing for the next fifty years."
-- Robert S. McNamara, 1967

"As the greatest power on earth, the United States had the power to lose face, the power to admit error, and the

power to act with magnanimity."
-- James Thomson

"Each $1 worth of damage inflicted on North Vietnam cost the United States $9.60."
-- CIA report on Vietnam bombing

"One Britisher is as good as ten Japanese but unfortunately there are eleven Japs."
-- British soldier, Singapore 1941 quoted by Cecil Brown, *Suez to Singapore*

"Go tell the Spartans, stranger passing by, that here obedient to their laws we lie."
-- Greek epitaph, battle of Thermopylae

"Withdrawal of combat troops is a strange way to win a war, or even to force the way to a favorable settlement. Once started, it could not easily be halted and would, like escalation, build its own momentum and, as forces dwindled, become irreversible."
-- Barbara Tuchman, *The March of Folly*

"Because war is controlled by its political object, the value of this object must determine the sacrifices to be made for it, both in magnitude and also in duration. Once the expenditure of effort exceeds the value of the political object, the object must be renounced . . . "
-- Harry G. Summers, quoting Karl von Clausewitz

"We must be clear sighted in beginnings, for, as in their budding we discern not the danger, so in their full growth we perceive not the remedy."
-- Montaigne

"Congress will not accept any responsibility for a 'crash landing' unless it has been in on the 'takeoff'."
-- Lyndon Johnson

"Once on the tiger's back it is very hard to pick the place to dismount."
-- George Ball

"Once you put that first soldier ashore you never know how many others are going to follow him."
-- General Maxwell Taylor

"The difference between results and consequences is that results are what you expect and consequences are what you get."
-- Robert S. McNamara

"You must either get excited, get passionate, fight and get it over with, or pull out. It's unbelievably hard to fight a limited war."
-- Lady Bird Johnson, on Vietnam

"Military force - especially when wielded by an outside power - cannot bring order in a country that cannot govern itself. External military force cannot substitute for the political order and stability that must be forged by a people for themselves."
-- Robert S. McNamara

"War is essentially the triumph, not of one weapon over another...but of one will over another."
-- General Sir Ian Hamilton

"If you know your enemies and know yourself, you can win a hundred battles without a single loss. If you know only yourself but not your opponent, you may win or you may lose. If you know neither yourself nor your enemy, you will almost certainly lose."
-- Sun Tzu, *The Art of War*

"Perpetual peace is a dream. War is an element of the divine order of the world. In it are developed the noblest virtues of men: courage and self-denial, fidelity to duty, and the spirit of sacrifice . . . without war, the world would stagnate and lose itself in materialism."
-- Helmuth von Moltke

"It may be that when there is no violent conflict, there is no progress."
-- V.K. Krishna Menon

Timeless Quotes

5

History and Science

"If this is a battle of wits, they're sending in someone who's unarmed."
-- John Lowe, trial lawyer quoted by Peter Matthiessen, *In the Spirit of Crazy Horse*

"In the unfolding pageant of history no event is isolated."
-- Edward Peplow

"Throughout history all human accomplishment has depended on a combination of the four types of men – The Ambitious, The Man of Action, The Thinker, The Idealist."
-- Edward Peplow

"Time has its revolutions – there must be a period and an end to all temporal things, *finis rerum*, an end of names and dignities and whatsoever is of this earth. They are entombed in the urns and sepulchers of mortality."
-- Sir Randolph Crew

"History does not long entrust the care of freedom to the weak or the timid."
-- Dwight D. Eisenhower, First Inaugural

"Never give in, never give in, never, never, never, never, in nothing, great or small, large or petty, never give in except to convictions of honor and good sense."
-- Winston Churchill

"If you are going through hell, keep going."
-- Winston Churchill

"All the forces in the world are not so powerful as an idea whose time has come."
-- Victor Hugo

"He has all of the virtues I dislike and none of the vices I admire."
-- Winston Churchill

"He is a very modest man and has every right to be."
-- Winston Churchill

Timeless Quotes

"Success consists of going from failure to failure without the loss of enthusiasm."
-- Winston Churchill

"I do not want men of intelligence - I want men of brutality."
-- Adolf Hitler

"The only thing new in this world is the history you don't know."
-- Harry S. Truman

"Do you really believe that the sciences would ever have originated and grown if the way had not been prepared by magicians, alchemists, astrologers and witches . . . ?"
-- Friederich Wilhelm Nietzsche

"The past is a foreign country; they do things differently there."
-- L.P. Hartley

"I have a tremendous admiration for Caesar. But . . . I myself belong rather to the class of Bismarcks."
-- Mussolini

"Diverse paths lead diverse folk the right way to Rome."
-- Chaucer

"I fired him because he wouldn't respect the authority of the President. That's the answer to that. I didn't fire him because he was a dumb son of a bitch, although he was, but that's not against the law for generals. If it was, half to three-quarters of them would be in jail."
-- Harry S. Truman on removing MacArthur

"History is written by the winners."
-- Alex Haley

"Hitler was a reverse King Midas - everything he touched was transformed not into gold but into corpses."
-- Albert Speer

"If prison is not the University of Crime, it is at least the University of Moral Corruption."
-- Albert Speer

"When the Seleucid king Antiochus attacked Egypt in 168 BC, the Roman ambassador Popillius Laenas told the king to withdraw. When the king asked for more time to consider this, the ambassador drew a circle in the sand around the king and told him he could leave it once he had decided. The king considered the implications of this original 'line drawn in the sand', and backed down."
-- Philip Matyszak, *Chronicle of the Roman Republic*

"With the defeat of the Reich, there will remain in the world only two great powers capable of confronting each other - the United States and Soviet Russia. The laws of both history and geography will inevitably compel these two powers to a trial of strength . . . "
-- Adolf Hitler, April 2, 1945

"Loyalty is really in fact a bad thing, for it always presupposes a certain ethical blindness on the part of the loyal person. If someone really knew what was good and what was evil, loyalty would go by the board. There is only one valid kind of loyalty - loyalty to morality."
-- Albert Speer

"What we learn from history is that men do not learn from history."
 -- L. Sprague de Camp, paraphrasing Hegel

"Egyptian kings married their own sisters, under the pretext that Ptolemaic royal blood was too divine to mingle with that of mere mortals . . . "
-- L. Sprague de Camp, *Great Cities of the Ancient World*

"The curious thing about science in Alexandria is that it accomplished so much - and then stopped . . . science, however, must compete for attention, belief, respect, interest, and financial support with politics, commerce, art, literature, religion, entertainment, sport, war, and all the other activities of men. If one of these interests greatly expands its appeal to the people, it does so at the expense of the others . . . "
-- L. Sprague de Camp

"Of the mass religions, Christianity made the most effective use of the new principles. Having the tightest organization, the most bewildering logic, the most impressive sacred literature, and the most fanatical spirit of any, it captured the Roman Imperial government; then, armed with the terrifying doctrines of exclusive salvation, eternal damnation, and the imminent end of the world, and backed by the Roman Emperor's executioner, it soon swept its rivals from the board . . . "
-- L. Sprague de Camp, *Cities of the Ancient World*

"Whenever Romans were at their most ruthless and decadent, they conquered the Mediterranean world. When their conduct improved, the barbarians conquered them..."
-- L. Sprague de Camp, *Cities of the Ancient World*

Timeless Quotes

"Every government, whether democratic, oligarchic, or monarchist, has two duties, both of which must in some measure be performed if it is to remain in being. The community must be safeguarded against enemies from without, and its members must be protected against maltreatment from within. The former is achieved by arms, the latter by laws . . . "
-- Roman emperor Justinian, quoted by L. Sprague de Camp, *Cities of the Ancient World*

"Prison does not silence ideas whose time has come."
-- Barbara Tuchman, *The March of Folly*

"If man could learn from history, what lessons it might teach us! But passions and party blind our eyes, and the light which experience gives us is a lantern on the stern which shines only on the waves behind us."
-- Samuel Coleridge

"The Africans had no wheeled transport and...no animal transport either; they had no roads nor towns; no tools except small hand hoes, axes, wooden digging sticks, and the like; no manufactures, and no industrial products except the simplest domestic handiwork; no commerce as we understand it and no currency, although in some places barter of produce was facilitated by the use of small shells; they had never heard of working for wages. They went stark naked or clad in bark of trees or skins of animals; and they had no means of writing, even by

hieroglyphics, nor by numbering except by their fingers or making notches in a stick or knots in a piece of grass or fibre; they had no weights or measures of general use. Perhaps most astonishing of all to the modern European mind they had no calendar or notation of time . . . They were pagan, spirit or ancestor propitiators in the grip of magic or witchcraft, their minds cribbed and confined by superstition . . . They are a people who in 1890 were in a more primitive condition than anything of which there is any record in pre-Roman Britain."
-- Sir Philip Mitchell, former governor of British East Africa, 1890

"Use all means to persuade the Apaches or any other tribe to come in for the purpose of making peace, and when you get them together kill all the grown Indians and take the children prisoners and sell them to defray the expense of killing the Indians . . . "
-- Colonel John R. Baylor, proclamation to CSA troops, 1862

"We did not ask you white men to come here. The Great Spirit gave us this country as a home. You had yours. We did not interfere with you. The Great Spirit gave us plenty of land to live on, and buffalo, deer, antelope and other game. But you have come here; you are taking my land from me; you are killing off our game, so it is hard for us to live. Now, you tell us to work for a living, but the Great Spirit did not make us to work but to live by hunting. You

white men can work if you want to. We do not interfere with you, and again you say, why do you not become civilized? We do want your civilization! We would live as our fathers did and their fathers before them."
-- Chief Crazy Horse, Lakota Sioux, *c.*1875

6

Business and Commerce

"The real bottom line is in heaven."
-- Edwin Land

"It was a friendship founded on business, which is far better than a business founded on friendship."
-- John D. Rockefeller

"Business and pleasure don't mix – likewise business and idealism."
-- Anon

"You can only tell who's been swimming naked when the tide goes out."
-- Warren Buffett

"The specialist learns more and more about less and less until, finally, he knows everything about nothing; while the generalist learns less and less about more and more until, finally, he knows nothing about everything."
-- Anon

"Marketing is simply sales with a college education."
-- John Freund

"When you've got them by the wallet, their hearts and minds will follow."
-- Verne Naito

"We are very different from the rest of the world. Our only natural resource is the hard work of our people."
-- Japanese executive

"America is the land of opportunity if you're a businessman in Japan."
-- Lawrence Peter

"Final offer: something a veteran negotiator makes just prior to making concessions."
-- Fisk and Barron, *Great Business Quotations*

"To succeed in the world one should seem a fool but be wise."
-- Charles de Montesquieu

"Nothing succeeds like success."
-- Alexander Dumas

"Nothing succeeds like one's own successor."
-- Anon

"All you need in life is ignorance and confidence, and then success is sure."
-- Mark Twain

"I cannot give you a formula for success, but I give you the formula for failure: try to please everybody."
-- Herbert Swope

"The classic formula for success is: Dress British, Think Yiddish."
-- Jim Fisk, *Great Business Quotations*

"Leaders don't create followers, they create more leaders."
-- Anon

"Great leaders don't blame the tools they are given. They work to sharpen them."
-- Simon Sinek

"One an organization loses its spirit of pioneering and rests on its early work, its progress stops."
-- Thomas J. Watson

"A good leader is someone who takes a little more than his share of the blame, and a little less than his share of the credit."
-- Anon

"The meek may inherit the earth but not its mineral rights."
-- John Paul Getty

"Buy low, sell high, collect early, pay late."
-- Dick Levin

"Pioneering don't pay."
-- Andrew Carnegie

"No man ever yet became great by imitation."
-- Samuel Johnson

"Whatever is not nailed down is mine. Whatever I can pry loose is not nailed down."
-- Colis Huntington

"You have undertaken to cheat me. I will not sue you, for the law takes too long. I will ruin you."
-- Cornelius Vanderbilt

"Litigation is the basic legal right which guarantees every corporation its decade in court."
-- David Porter

"I don't want a lawyer to tell me what I cannot do. I want one to tell me how to do what I want to do."
-- J.P. Morgan

"Money is a good servant but a bad master."
-- H.G. Bohn

"One who thinks money can do everything is likely to do anything for money."
-- Hasidic proverb

"Corporation: an ingenious device for obtaining individual profit without individual responsibility."
-- Ambrose Bierce

"Most corporate executives have no idea what it means to earn a buck or make a payroll. They never see cash coming in. They are playing Monopoly."
-- Robert Levinson

"In all recorded history there has not been one economist who had to worry about where the next meal came from."
-- Peter Drucker

"It's always capabilities, not intentions that matter the most."
-- Anon

"There are three ways to work on a project:
1. Faster
2. Better
3. Cheaper

Any two, but *only* two will work."
-- Anon

"The odds of something happening boil down to:
a) Probable
b) Reasonably Possible
c) Remote"
-- Anon

"A compromise is an agreement whereby both parties get what neither of them wanted."
-- Anon

"Control your own destiny or someone else will."
-- Jack Welch

"You can delegate authority but not responsibility."
-- Stephen W. Comiskey

"Your most unhappy customers are your greatest source of learning."
-- Bill Gates

"A man will succeed at anything about which he is really enthusiastic."
-- Charles M. Schwab

"I try to buy stock in businesses that are so wonderful that even an idiot can run them - because sooner or later, one will."
-- Warren Buffett

"Work expands so as to fill the time available for its completion."
-- C. Northcote Parkinson

"The closest to perfection a person ever comes is when he fills out a job application."
-- Stanley Randall

"Murphy's Laws
1. If it wasn't for the last minute, nothing would get done.
2. Once a job is fouled up, anything done to improve it makes it worse.
3. Don't be irreplaceable. If you can't be replaced, you can't be promoted.
4. Machines that have broken down will work perfectly when the repairman arrives.
5. When the bosses talk about improving productivity, they are never talking about themselves.

6. If someone says he will do something "without fail", he won't.
7. There is never enough time to do it right the first time, but there is always enough time to do it over.
8. The last person to quit or was fired will be held responsible for everything that goes wrong, until the next person quits or is fired.
9. Never ask two questions in a business letter. The reply will discuss the one in which you are least interested, and say nothing about the other.
10. Success is a matter of luck; just ask any failure.
11. If you can't get your work done in 24 hours, work nights.
12. The more pretentious the corporate name, the smaller the organization. For example, *The Murphy Center for Codification of Human and Organization Law*, contrasted to *IBM, GM, GE, AT&T*.
13. Important letters which contain no errors will develop errors in the mail.
14. The more crap you put up with, the more crap you are going to get.
15. There will always be beer cans rolling on the floor of the car when the boss asks you for a ride home from the office."

-- Anon

"You're moving backward if you're not moving forward."
-- Anon

"Change is inevitable. Growth is optional."
-- Cindy Rutz

"An organization functions best when there is a shortage of personnel. When there is a surplus, many are fighting for more responsibility and more people to justify their position and promotion rather than concentrating on their work. Voluminous papers are written and passed from desk to desk as substitutes for just getting the job done."
-- K.D. Nichols, Major General U.S.A. Ret.

"Whenever you hear someone say 'it's not the money, it's the principle' - it's the money"
-- Anon

"Management is doing things right; leadership is doing the right thing."
-- Peter Drucker

"Be willing to make decisions. That's the most important quality in a good leader."
-- T. Boone Pickens

"Sometimes you make the right decision; sometimes you make the decision right."
-- Dr. Phil McGraw

"Be nice to nerds. Chances are you'll end up working for one."
-- Bill Gates

"The harder you work, the luckier you get."
-- Gary Player

"Success is never final but failure can be."
-- Bill Parcells

"You can't build a reputation on what you are going to do."
-- Henry Ford

"I have not failed. I've just found 10,000 ways that won't work."
-- Thomas A. Edison

"People are not the most important asset. The right people are."
-- Jim Collins

"Face reality as it is, not as it was or as you wish it to be."
-- Jack Welsh

"It takes 20 years to build a reputation and five minutes to ruin it."
-- Warren Buffet

Timeless Quotes

"You can't stumble if you're not in motion..."
-- Richard Carlton, engineer at 3M

"How, after all, are you able to evaluate the inner workings of people around you, and eventually understand them and know them for what they are? You do so through your observation of these three outward signs: the things they do, the way they act when things happen to them, and their reasons for doing things. In other words, you judge people by their actions, reactions, and motivations."
-- Scott Meredith

"As one Southern Publisher famously confessed, 'I owe my exalted position in life to two great American institutions - nepotism and monopoly.' "
-- Related by Warren Buffett

'Promotion seduces men's judgment and produces compliance,"
-- B.H. Liddell Hart

"Nothing succeeds like failure. The crucified Christ became more potent than the living one. We remember Hannibal, Napoleon, Robert E. Lee and Rommel more than the generals who defeated them."
-- B.H. Liddell Hart

"If you want to know whether you are destined to be a success or failure in life, you can easily find out. The test is simple, and it is infallible. Are you able to save money? If not, drop out. You will lose . . . "
-- James J. Hill, Minnesota railroad tycoon

"Rule number one: Never lose money. Rule number two: Never forget number one."
-- Warren Buffett

"No, no, no - a hungry hound hunts best . . . "
-- Mine owner James Fair, to his partners when vetoing a raise for a valuable employee

"A man who can't afford to lose should never sit in a poker game."
-- James Fair

"The first son is the heir, the second son is the spare."
-- Anon

"The elevator to success is out of order. You'll have to use the stairs . . . one step at a time."
-- Joe Girard

"The man who has confidence in himself gains the confidence of others."
-- Hasidic Proverb

"For anybody looking for a job there is a considerable difference between 49 and 51."
-- John Gunther

"If you have nothing to do, don't do it here."
-- Sign in shop, Kenya, Africa

"Impossibilium nulla obligatio est."
-- Roman law, "The impossible is never required."

"De minimis non curat lex."
-- Roman law, "The law takes no account of trifles."

"Nemo dat quod non habet."
-- Roman law, "No one can give what he does not have."

THE AUTHOR

JIM REDMAN spent over 35 years living in California before semi-retiring to Arizona in 2004. During his professional career he served as CEO of a diversified industrial firm, and as CEO of a publicly traded company that did crisis management consulting for clients in various industries.

He is the author of *The World According to Max*; *Searching for Jacob Waltz*; *For Conspicuous Gallantry: Remembering James Stockdale*; and *Last Stage West: The Wickenburg Massacre*. He divides his time now between client assignments, researching material for writing projects, and exploring the Sonoran Desert.

Jim Redman

Timeless Quotes

Made in the USA
Columbia, SC
27 April 2018